Praise for *Essay Poems*

Essay Poems is Donald Wellman's most ambitious volume of poetry to date. The verses absorb everything including several languages besides English (Spanish, Latin, German, French). His poetry evokes the universe seen from the all-encompassing point of view of Borges' Aleph. The center slips away. There is no sense of personal identity. But someone emerges, with a liquid body. Information, quotations agglomerate and turn around in a dancing vortex propelled by a *horror vacui*. Allusions dart in every direction as the richness of the text overwhelms the reader.   – ROBERTO ECHAVARREN

Wellman is a wanderer, a wonderer, and well of knowledge, too. Probing, disturbing, disorienting, and melancholic, these are erudite and emotional essay-poem-collages. They loop and spin the reader in multiple directions from the mucilaginous body to fishing with handline and hook, or searching for a whisk in a Chinese store, a storm of stars, the throes of love, the self is felt, reflected, distorted, and imagined.   – ROS ZIMMERMANN

These serial poems point the reader toward unexpected affinities between text and text, event and consequence, thought and being. Wellman's enormous erudition penetrates into the essence of what matters in life and in the life of the mind. In the hands of a lesser poet, such an ambitious sweep would be doomed to fail: Wellman triumphs. – CHRISTOPHER SAWYER-LAUÇANNO

Wellman's methodical *chora*, offering a unique philosophical-spiritual and literary approach, is a marvelously intelligent translation "of false / and fictionalized confessions," beautifully wrought and suffused with a rueful gaiety that will break your heart. "A passageway to a parallel world," everything one might fear and desire: dick, Zyklon B, resemblances, contiguities, and causations "between thought and prayer" can be found herein, one of the most compelling books you will ever read.   – ANDREW LEVY

A finely crafted, bawdy, beautiful, heartrending and hilarious testament to the poetic vocation. Who would have suspected that the dick--not the Lacanian phallus but the humble dick, pink and shriveled, "wrapped in folds of uncertainty," that "moldy wad... wound with red rubber bands"--could be the anchoring point of an elegiac mode? Only a poet of Wellman's craft and erudition, that ring in every phrase and every line.   – BILL LAVENDER

ESSAY POEMS

Donald Wellman

DOS MADRES

2017

DOS MADRES PRESS INC.
P.O.Box 294, Loveland, Ohio 45140
www.dosmadres.com   editor@dosmadres.com

Dos Madres is dedicated to the belief that the small press is essential to the vitality of contemporary literature as a carrier of the new voice, as well as the older, sometimes forgotten voices of the past. And in an ever more virtual world, to the creation of fine books pleasing to the eye and hand.

Dos Madres is named in honor of Vera Murphy and Libbie Hughes, the "Dos Madres" whose contributions have made this press possible.

Dos Madres Press, Inc. is an Ohio Not For Profit Corporation and a 501 (c) (3) qualified public charity. Contributions are tax deductible.

Executive Editor: Robert J. Murphy

Illustration & Book Design: Elizabeth H. Murphy
www.illusionstudios.net

Typeset in Adobe Garamond Pro
ISBN 978-1-939929-98-3
Library of Congress Control Number: 2017957519

First Edition

ACKNOWLEDGEMENTS

"χῶρος" and "φύση" at *Talisman a Journal of Contemporary Poetry and Poetics*, #45.

"Philadelphia," *Dispatches* (Sept. 5, 2017).

"Ejaculatory" and "Dicks" (published as "Songs") at *BlazeVox* 16.

"God is Love" at *Journal of Poetics Research* 5.

"Monadology" at Annex Press.

"[What string cuts like an ice string?]," "[Donne and Eliot infiltrate]," "[The body of a woman on a butcher's slab]," and "[Where two tones approach]," *Golden Handcuffs Review*, vol. II, #24.

ESSAY POEMS AND EXERCISES

In constructing this book, I have been thinking about the English language serial poem from Jack Spicer to Lisa Robertson. Some of my poems sustain themselves over considerable lengths. Different forms of superposition insert vertical dimensions into the flow of the text. For H.D. these layers were palimpsestic. For Gilles Deleuze and Félix Guattari these planes are filaments of desiring production. Other forces form liquid or lubricating layers between associated planes. Meaning appears to be suspended. Disorientation affects development at multiple turnings. If the energy of composition sustains itself, even though as a result of multiplication, a poem may not articulate a satisfying conclusion, still, by other lights, it may feel complete, erotic, nostalgic, melancholic. Some of these poems are translinguistic. Others sacred. Their address to corporeality, raw.

Contents

Part 1

In work with handline and hook,

as in poetry, variation

and device

produce

design.

Perception warps

rhythmic fall.

Interval? Indolence?

Blinding shadows

on ocean floor.

Lo the barb glints with subterfuge,

catches fisherman and prey.

Molar molecularity.

"This is just to say."

It's on my mind to leave some words

to distinguish

between thought and prayer

A ridgeline within fog

A garnet among amethysts

Not a god among stars

immanence is not transformation,

smoke within wood.

A page wanting inscription

is written upon.

Death within flesh.

Two substances reveal a third.

Is harmony immanent to noise?

Chaos is before creation.

Time is immanent to star dust.

Sadness within defeated

soldiers. Loss haunts their lives.

His body, immanent to mine,

a grandfather and son,

an idea within an idea.

A daughter in my belly.

EJACULATORY

My interior monologs go on and on and on as in a dream of which I am aware although sleeping, and it continues gnawing. I stand outside myself. As I am your guest, I want to say what I have to say and in saying it I will try not to break stride or lose my composure.

DICKS

He hews to a faith in absolute rhythm. He decided
each line must be as long or as short as it is.
For recreation he follows a site that provides
Bollywood commentary, Absolute_Rhythm.com, se dice.
His life once took him to a room in Vedado.
where his thought unwinds. He is writing an elegy
on the death of his uncle, cleft palate and wandering eye,
who dragged one foot in the roadside gutter, looking for coins.
After prison and exile, he succumbed to AIDS.
Spring arrived early that winter
that was not a winter. His Cuba, a fantasy of escape
to a warm place. He was unable to return
despite climate change. This is an elegy for Reinaldo Arenas.
A view to the sea at the foot of the street, a torn curtain,
lace balloons on the wind, the surf races over open water
before it crashes against the Malecón.
The room holds the existential loneliness
familiar from paintings by Hopper.
Walker Evans photographed Maine interiors
after returning from Havana,
the sooty face of a dockworker
who refused to submit because an American President had
                                        [chosen to visit.
His childhood girlfriend's stepfather owned a sugar refinery
now the fields are overgrown, production has ceased, children
                                        [eat mealy worms.
Large-scale cultivation of algae is planned. Seething mats
of biological matter decay in lagoons, words and breath,
assemble the inaugural rhythm. A prenatal island
theorized by Maria Zambrano.
The wind brisk, on the north shore.
This is for poets who drift into allegory.

It's a jumble of personae.
This is for Michael Thompson whose uncut dick haunts
my work.
Music is not photographs.
This is for girls with dicks who love girls with dicks.
Men go by. Go, bye!

On the road to the precipice, his feet drag, catching on the
                                                    [twiggy brown stuff.
He remembers the contagious hospital. Gulls float above the
                                                    [distant lake,
the sky empyrean blue. In youth his head
had hung over the edge of a cliff in Kentucky,
sandy hair floated on the updraft
from furnaces below. Other boys
had chased him under the schoolyard fence
and out onto a sandy plain where turtles bred.
His own adenoidal voice haunted him. Clarissa had been
surprised at how well he knew his times tables.
In the limestone caves he felt her tresses on his hairless chest.
He counted holding his breath until he found relief.
They lived in Goldville. His mother refused his father's advances.
Red mud washes in under the front door and out the back.
His oedipal fantasies center on his father's dick.
The radio of a 52 Ford Fairlane brayed "Love me Tender. Do,"
Be gentle he prayed. My name is Pam.

Born for redemption, his grandmother combs his hair,
her fingers, polished ivory. She pours molten nickel on his eyelids.

6

Her sister owned utensils of gleaming gold:
nut pickers, tweezers. The dog slept on the Persian carpet.
The spiral stairs serve no purpose. A recursive
ritual keeps turning him back
to the uninitiated swamp. On a winter's night
Jupiter rides on the rim of a nearly full moon.
Looking upwards he loses his balance. No lawn, no dog
to secure salvific rescue. He lay there.
Icy cold snakes nibble his feet.
His dick got hard. His daughter's friends
are having their first babies.
The vision transports him as if he were the Virgin Mary.
Ascending among the clouds, he promises redemption
to those who sought. Genet
wrote, "they were winged and puffy and big,
sober as cherubs, splendid dicks,
made of barley–sugar."

Some towns have no sky, daylight harsh like acid,
lichen in groomed symbiosis. He taught the pupils
to cry and express love. He was mocked. Their parents,
they knew, had lung cancer and bowel cancer. It was
the hand of God. They'd blink, afraid of being swatted.
These were God's people, resistant to change,
mistrusting those who promoted tolerance.
The boys aspired to serve in the fire brigade or with
the nigger-hating cops. The flags with red fields, boots laced
with horizontal red bars in KKK memoriam promise
extermination to those
who opposed their will. His heart glowed
with neon rage as Dylann Roof plotted revenge

for the poverty his parents extolled.
The teacher knew the hatred and scorn
in which the élèves held his values. He died
a poet and Oscar Wilde scholar, recipient
of degrading evaluations, valiant in hypocrisy,
exhausted when his lungs too gave out, crooning
Sanskrit mantras and bowing his head with a private
fatalism, his prostrate oozing blood,
his dick limp, a soggy rope.

How detach a soul from its reality? A form of sufferance,
he found in reading Gogol. Souls need not
be understood as transcendental objects, packed
in crates of celestial milk. Flesh
speaks to callouses, sweat, and urine. Wisdom
causes bones to ache. The poet imagines children at the backdoor
or their shadows. Breakfast, always granola, toast, and coffee.
Then he tended to his messages. Deleted most.
He had no sense of an audience to whom
his words might have better been addressed.
He honed his sentences and hoped they would read well
after his death. He no longer smokes. Restlessness
each afternoon took him to a gym where he ran and pushed
his limbs against selected weights. He contemplates
the rationalized body, a diagram of different
cuts of meat. At times he learns from television
of suffering, hunger, fear or drowning amid
the obstinate Greek Isles. He understood the agony
of border crossings over frozen beet fields,
his reality in the days of feeling a thigh
pressed against his, in a clubroom in Schwäbisch Gemund.

His dick grew hard gazing upon a pockmarked face,
solicitous eyes, mascara, the boy's sour breath
repellant to his priggish sense of self-worth.
A woman he'd met in Aachen studied like him
the poetry of *West Indies, Ltd.* Both dreamed
of African dick. At dawn they saw the Eta Aquarids,
fragments of Halley's comet, spermatic droplets.
5 May 2000. Dead souls! ha! He nodded off again.

"And the swallows obeyed his voice," one tract records.
The brothers who followed him dispersed
to the four corners of the world. On my patio,
the preferred nesting ground is the cover
of the porch light, a sheltered nook. The sun
turns the breasts of the little birds orange.
Lime drenched stalactites adhere to the walls.
St. Minna gave his cloak to a mendicant.
A quail once mistook the glass of a sliding door
for a passageway to a parallel world.
Misha's dad, after he had converted to Judaism,
contemplated circumcision for his adolescent son.
His flesh most tender when baked with pepper
and butter. When Joel died, a white dove
entered the church and sat upon a rafter
above the coffin as the shofar played. A man
who loved women was the theme of the eulogy.
Even in old age his dick was firm and luminescent.
[Misha was 13 on 2 March 2008].

Not the first to write about dicks and not a profligate,
he likened the penis to a moldy wad of stock certificates,
tightly wound with red rubber bands. A cross section
made with a surgical saw reveals layers of filaments,
some of spongey tissue, others, a thin mesh. Erection
results when different layers slide over one another, interior frottage,
and fill with blood. The ejection of little homunculi, each
with a perfect little dick serves propagation.
Females apparently have reproduced by sybaritic stimulation,
unless an angel intervene as was the case with Mother Mary.
Sister Victorine discharged her duties by striking his bare bum
with her ferule. All the children shrieked when they saw
the pink worm of his shriveled dick. I've been continent evermore.
It helped me contemplate when serving mass, caught
between going and not going, my eyes watered in prayer.

With Mephistophelean bushy brows,
the thrush swore all
women were vile. The swallow replied,
the male betrayed our lord.
Peter slept in fated sorrow.
Three times the cock had crown
without awakening the disciple.
On a cherub's lower lip,
a dollop of blood appeared.
A child in a white tuxedo
played a white violin. "In what sense
is this a poem?" Philomela protests,
"It reeks of senseless allegory.

"You claim to defend the weaker sex.
"The moral, as Mary is my witness,
"is that women will themselves defend
"their honor from the charms
"of deceitful men." From the mantel
where it stood, in the poet's chamber,
a cock of phallic jade swore to the assembled guests,
"Bi his holi name,
"Ne shal I neuere suggen shame
"Bi maidnes ne bi wiue."
Not every cock 's a dick.

The rhythmical creation of beauty is deadpan,
mathematicians agreed, citing the evolution
of complex constructions capable of reproduction.
Voices outside compared dogs that had been
entered into the race. Pure possession exalts
rivalry. The butter left out turned rancid
but he used it in any case to prepare
pancakes for Easter breakfast. As a child
the day celebrated duties he had to pay.
Now everyone thinks about the marathon
and the violence of two years ago. He considers
how he's been able to adapt to his own
prosthetic devices, upper and lower plates
for mastication. When sucking dick, it's best
to remove these although some souls prefer
the excitation of dental drag. Languorous,
his preferred style, a precursor poet of language,
he mixed roles and orientations by whim.

Had I known this music, "Song of the Bees,"
I would have presented my *Roman Exercises* differently,
Amhrán na mBeach. I turn back often
to what I might have said. From the outset,
I had no desire to make an exhaustive
compendium. My method like that here
was to work with what comes to hand, observing
the order with which insight obtrudes
upon sense. The purpose, barring any planning
or premeditation, led me from page to page.
Within any passage, aporias of attention
embed themselves. Concatenation
is marked at every level of the whole
as it emerges, sloughing its skin, much like a snake
or a penis about to ejaculate. Rules entail
mobilizing anticipatory surprise. Satisfaction
requires an unexpected allusion as when
beestings raise welts on an engorged dick.
Exquisite tomes of melancholy surround me
in a world where poets carry on their backs
their grandfathers' cocks.

Mars prepares to enter retrograde. Another bomb
explodes. The beaches of Israel are bleak in winter.
Bombs in Lahore, Brussels, Côte d'Ivoire. In Zandvort
the young couple found shelter that Easter of homeless
travel, their private diaspora. Tension with her father
did not allow redress. He served nonetheless
as a specialist in helicopter repair parts. His mates

called him pussy. In the Hitler years his wife fretted
while her Marxist husband, to avoid capture, slept in vineyards.
He'd been a carpenter who roamed with gangs
in his Wanderjahr, "hat und stock, aber mutter
weint so schwer." His parents cried for him.
The soldier's brother sought the mysterious Mine Falls
where salmon gleamed. Thoreau inventoried
that island "observed the bittern probe the mud for its food."
Brothers in their bed wrestled with desire, the dick
of one impaled the other. Death's unremitting
melancholy sapped the strength of the victor.

Certain feelings began to inhabit him. "Rescue gave way to love."
Multiple and varied though emotions were, a core identity
withstood the flood. Or conversely,
the center did not hold, but slipped away. Rescue imposed
an obligation to return the affection that triggered sorrow.
"An impulse to action sings
of a semblance of things related as equated."
What is a self-identical idea?
Does it impute to essence the ability to recognize itself. The sensitive
subject is also the sensitive object of desire. I am me, as it were.
"I is not I" ever. Does editing for precision turn words into poetry?
Or does essence reside in the perception of form,
no matter if ungainly or cluttered.
The arrangement of lines upon the page may be instructive in this
less musical age. He began to doubt
if he had read Husserl in his youth.
His brother insisted otherwise. In Freiberg and in Davos
he lay long in bed writing to his soulmate
with gratitude for self-discovery,
"the friend whom he desired." Adolescent woe

does not understand the object of its lust. Emilio punished
his dick, relieved to unburden himself so.

Of his tortured soul Georg Trakl wrote, "magnetic whips of light
lacerate the walls." Unnerved by his sister's comeliness,
he fell to his knees. A purple flame drowned in his mouth.
It's unspeakable, God, that man be so humbled in his prime.
I wrote of a simulacrum or image, of an image of an image,
a conversion of forces from whence the soul springs,
a singularized immanence that inspires and resolves.
In "The Virgin Mountain," are embedded references
to Gilles Deleuze who imposed a masturbatorium on the schematic
of the house that is an image of the world where children
grow into maturity without inhibition. A principle
like this may have resolved a brother's love for his sister.
Would Trakl's "dark flutes of autumn" still follow
their path toward extermination in death camps
where devout Jews feared contamination
but were unable to refrain from fondling their dicks
before clouds of Zyklon B made poetry impossible.

"Amid sparks from the whirlwind, the Japanese warrior asks
for silence," wrote Lezama Lima.
"They respond to him, during the descent into the inferno,
bones pissed on with blood by the enraged Mexican god."[31]
The writer explores beastliness by incorporating it. The poem
does away with language. Indeed, poets of both sexes
can use their dicks to douse a fire. Paris 1964,
Carolee Schneemann produced "Meat Joy."

Birds and fish and sausages instead of dicks.
The troupe revels in erotic play: red ink and a chalky resin,
yards of cotton swaddling and tissue transform the scene
into a lunar meadow of floating forms.

Are "sex" and "play" convertible joys? Coins copulate,
Rilke imagined in his night terrors. Roger Caillois defines play
"as free, separate, uncertain, and unproductive, yet regulated
and make-believe." Our video games
exact their toll, transforming meat joy into war.
The dick itself, a substitute or simulacrum for the phantom body
that is spawned in Hollywood–haunted dreams. If it error be
to speak of woman as I have done, put me down as a misogynist
who reverences the female dick (theorized by Judith Butler).
In any case, I have called a dick a dick. It's a game
of 'fort-da' that compels me to continue on and on and on.

Is this work a forgery? In one of her works, Pam Dick equates transcription
with commentary. And then claims, "But also trans lit could be expanded be-
yond intertextual adventures." My thought occupies the bodies of those who
appear between the lines. As often as I use the word "dick" in this poem, I refer
to personages who have dominated my phenomenological life. See: Traver Pam
Dick, *Eoagh*, Oct. 15, 2011.

Part 2

A void tunnels wormwise

through a block of percepts and affects.

Becoming endures

in the dematerialized work of art.

LIVES OF THE POETS

My beloved Emilio did not study with Husserl, he says.
He was a student in Freiburg then. Instead
he courted solitude and dreamed of the boy who inspired him
to study animal husbandry. "Entre cañones,"
Antonio perished in the Battle for Madrid.

My grim Antonio of another age learned his Latin
from Augustinians who employed
corporal punishment for wayward boys.
The donkey screamed when the soldier bashed in its brains.
Now in his old age, his daughters and his granddaughter
[comfort him.

The nun with a concertina regaled the girls
who skipped rope in the alley. In those days
the sexes did not mix during recess. The boys
gambled with marbles or threw pennies
against a wall. The poet's glasses like saucers.

Donald loved languages. Gerard who wrote
in sprung rhythm. Donald venerated James
who skulked among statues and fingered
the anus of Venus. "Silver apples of the moon,"
he lived in a garage with an earthen floor.

The linoleum reeked of axel grease and horse manure.
Among his books were Rabelais. In adolescence he
had walked along the Rhone where mustard bloomed.
He knew a Russian song about the margin of the sea.
His Rimbaud revelry befell upon a Neckar river barge.

He saw the Camargue with his adolescent daughter
They slept in the cloister. "Not by usura St Trophime."
Orange soda in the Night Café. Ireland and Spain,
long after inspiration had bent his bones into walking canes.
Grim, his love for solitude prepared him for eternity.

Clichés like milkweed float among embroideries.
It's not a poem about a "crumb of dust" as Edward Taylor
wrote, but of triumph for all its jags and jars. In the windy
blue Canadian air he climbed to the rooftop
and swept old carbon from the chimney flue.

Herman Melville suspends philosophers' skulls
from the yardarm of his Pequod. Stateless anomie,
my fisher king, not the seaport *polis*, where poets' children
thrive in a park above harbor tides. In Australian desert,
maternal men celebrate fatherhood, Bob, Allen, John.

After the loss of his eye, his family moved to West Acton
where the train to Fitchburg paused. My grandmother
took me to the Eye and Ear on the Nashua line.
A Woolworths in Scollay Sq. brilliant with plastic airplanes,
French toast slathered with chemical syrup. John?

Do you remember, Harvard Gardens in mystical '55.
Stephen and Robin and Jack. "No one listens to poetry."
I'm just back from the home on Dana St. where Charley,
who always wore farmer's jeans, waits for Mitzel.
In the parking lot, old men smoke salvaged butt ends.

A poetry collective is a tender memory. We met
on Bromfield Street, we met in Christiansted
and in the afterlife on the north shore of Haiti.
Bombs where poets gathered, Baghdad and Boston,
headlines in *El Pais*, rentboys that lonely summer.

Spain like New England, where lives are never
as they seem to those who seek the genuine article,
love in the antique mall, graves unmarked.
"Kids who die" is my subject, as it was Langston's.
Men of many hues, an international tribe.

Where lie the mothers in the plethora of lives?
Hermione and H.D. Fictive and real? In the snows
of yesteryear are Margarete and Gertrude.
Suzanne of Martinique, Elena's Tina Modotti, Djuna
who roams the world in search of home and hope?

My school of exile is a form of men and women,
adolescent intrusions, as this document shows. A common
frailty among old men. The frothy brew of my exuberance
leaves me nonplussed before the need to write and weave
citations into my text. A habit of my Aunt Gladys.

Her silver curls, her mirror and brush of plated gold. Margaret
asks how I survived our family life, our dad's cannibalistic rage.
Exile from the mills was easy enough for me.
First a coffin maker and then a professor.
The dissident Thoreau is my contemporary.

I hunted the condemned father, as was the case with Neil.
The mark of Cain on my brow. More kin to Grendel
than the hero, I wandered marshlands and botanized
flesh-eating plants, sinkholes that swallowed
cattle. My Irish bog, my mother's native land. Wo weilest du?

The boy held an owl in his eyes.

The skin over the flat bridge of his nose freckled,

he had no chin.

With the passage of years identity dissolves in the flat

[blue light

that mesmerizes a proud house on the high street.

Memory searches for his name,

surprised at how easily it rejects so many

before settling like a bird of prey

on one.

I wondered too about the becoming bird or animal

in the life of the boy. Acrid flecks of tobacco,

bitter on the lower lip,

and the rowdy wrestling among the strong.

I sat outside the ring watching

the erotic display that displaced the anger

that constricts the throat in the name of the father.

In the loft exposed beams provided nooks

for pigeons to roost.

Bird shit bred worms

that infected the mattress

where we lay in our love making,

his dick pressed against my anus.

All around the barn now and along the fence line

a shocking display of forsythia

ignites the very bowels

of beauty. Joy

is caught

on the wing of this light.

An uncanny face or simulacrum,

Medusa reversed, it might be a petrifaction?

A boiled and preserved New Guinea trophy

("vielleicht shrumpft gerade hier das Medusen haupt").

Faciality is divine and duplicitous.

Faciality is a trait of Jean Dubufet. Philosophy

requires the face of the interlocutor.

Poetry converses with that person within you

who looks on from outside.

MONADOLOGY

Invoking cells and colonies, the architect considered
the cathedral's structural integrity,
an apocalyptic framing of solar scales.[1]
Temples are monads, monads temples
where oversized horseflies awaken the first day of summer.
"The Capilla del Altillo is a rhomboid,
its roof, a hyperbolic paraboloid. Arcs
intersecting angles that spill over sun-bright
plazas, precisely indicated
shadows, enormous clocks, radial arms,
define solar scales" (*Prolog Pages* 94).
Subatomic particles will follow simultaneously
all possible paths.

The monad "uncurled from its cradle, or artichoke
globe."[2] Swimming monads abrupt
on oceans that were skies, skies oceans.
Maria Zambrano wrote about vegetables.

The vegetable dreams; its life is sleep. In it reality and dream are one, as in
fantasy, for it dreams itself. And also because it sleeps permanently and what it
dreams is what is. The plant is the shape of its dream. In the animal bad dreams
begin; the dream that is different from its own being, the nightmare. Night-
mare is the dream opposed to life. The dream that bears down on consciousness
or the hint of consciousness and that has to originate in the necessity for move-
ment. The quiet vegetable, ecstatic, is immersed in its sleep and in not moving
does not distinguish, between outside and inside. And so does not need to have
consciousness. Consciousness has risen from movement and the movement in
turn makes it feel and creates the sensation of a rift in its reality, divides it into
my "outside" and my "inside." Movement is necessary for the animal, it is the
generic form of its life, because its necessity is without limits. And because it
must go far in search of its satisfaction and this too is its power. Without move-
ment it has no power. And so the root of its necessity and the root of its power
equally oblige it to move. For the plant all must be felt inside, only gently may
it feel the outside and not as such, but as a brush, as a wound in the worst case.
The tree, the plant live their dream within, not only feeling the earth where its

roots are buried, but all of space, the dome of the sky. For these are born not in going out from itself, but in a budding; a passing from darkness to light, and the air that continues to cover them as before the earth did the seed, but without oppression; an inside very spacious and light where its being unfolds and enters through subtle relations with "the other," "the others," as with the animal. "The other" which is the origin of "the enemy." The feeling for other bodies will present itself to them in different forms of relation without struggle, or antagonism; corresponding perhaps to moments of contemplation of the beautiful in human life. The beautiful, even happiness devolves for man from the world where the vegetable has continued to live, since they bring it to the interior without boundaries. To a spacious "inside" where it is not imprisoned or exiled. To live outside is to wander in amazement and in struggle; to live inside is to be bound and isolated. This manner of vegetal living and that which man enjoys when he feels beauty or is happy, is neither outside nor inside; participation in the life of the whole, without going to find it; is the presence not pursued; the being without boundaries that senses the richness of the universe unfolded. Meanwhile in human life one seeks the whole of that which "the other" [el otro] and "the other" [lo otro] enclose within themselves, pursuing it, conquering it among the avatars of the necessity to possess what refuses us all the same, the quietude of living within and the freedom of living without. [3]

My mind slips into prelapsarian sludge.
By means of incorporation, the writer explores beastliness.
The experience of sex loses generic markers.
Aquamarine fish and arachnid presences,
a mucilaginous body, made of polysaccharide
carrageenan infests a plane of consistency.
He wanted to "stay in the dream arena."[4]
In a time before time that is not time,
alligators and lobsters, embedded in a tree,
weep a heavenly milk on which ants feed.
Scurrying feet swamp creation,
a red dye, acidic, ascetic to taste buds.

Every substance is a mirror of God.[5]
Foam in the wake of the barque,
an incessant dream of desperate poverty,
I drag two children over the pavement

27

away from police who inventory our belongings.
The yellow tape of no-return.

"It is not a flat plane hung before the eye like a window
but a glass float from a Japanese fishing net"[6]

Monads are incorporeal automatons (18)[7]
We fought over books. I chased the author over unstable crates
swathed in orange fabric that served as bridge or floating dock.
Milk, soap, milksop, as in a shopping list.
Of the bellybutton, my Roberto wrote,
of a bouncing dot with a bay and fierce blizzards that stung the
swaddled face,
"si mónada por rebote un punto más chico abandona para
volver a rebotar."
Spinning within spinning within blinding vortices,
subsumes space and vision.
Before nominating her father for the highest office in the land,
she depilated her vulva,
nervous lest she be exposed
as was my grandmother who in the end could only manage soft
and mushy food.
The vulva is a monad.

A soul cannot all at once open all its folds (81)
The death of the minotaur occurred within the cement gray
walls of the cellar.
Sackcloth covered the door,
"los sacos cubren la entrada del día"
There were no windows.
Sprinkles of blood decorate the chamber.
"Calmo el toro moribundo sosteniendo el sol bemol bala entre
acoplados corchetes de la incomunicable forma de su destrucción." [8]
Meat hooks. In Raul Zurita's *INRI*, from within a sphere

whose dimensions vary precipitously,
are heard sky and sunlight within the waves.
The monad is an eye that listens.
Sea and sky are tombs. Fish devour sky.[9]
Horizons subsumed within monads.
Roses spring from crowns of thorns
and fill the basins of the eyes.
The eye is a monad.

"Sea like sky falls into sky like ocean" in Bergval's *Drift* (58).
A monad within the shaking of the spheres
"coursing light packed ice melts
each passing monad"
Folded fabric, folded spheres.
"Layers if branches rub against one another."
Inside is only the irritation of not seeing
You push aside the branches
Shadows stick to your fingers.
"Quickly darkened your bite holds the trace"[10]

To tranquilize the black rhino
is now my theme
so that it may be transported by helicopter
across the savannah.

In empty rooms of dissonant thought, the thought of feeling you lay alongside
what you might be, of work, of unabsented being. Being small again. Every-
thing is cold and strange except you. You and your echo.[11] The pineal gland is a
walnut that focuses perception in Descartes measured world. Paul Klee wrote,
"I reflect on the innermost heart. I write the words on the forehead and round
the corners of the mouth. … If I were to paint a really truthful self-portrait,
you would see an odd shell. … Inside it would be myself, like the kernel in
a nut."[12] Symbols signify absences as if we were blind. Shadows are the time
signature of the Brownian motion of the soul.

There is therefore, nothing uncultivated, or sterile or dead ... no chaos, no confusion, save in appearances; somewhat as a pond would appear at a distance when we could see in it a confused movement, and so to speak, a swarming of the fish, without, however, discerning the fish themselves (69).

How were we to know that the translucent filaments were other than wrinkles in a watery world. Graminaceous entelechies with wheels. Did the conjoined monsters with several heads spewing literature and other substances gory and fiery, as proposed by Sir Edmund Spenser, obey the laws of good and evil?[13] Greater and lesser, the trajectories of the visible planets aligned in accord with projective meditation and deduction, as Descartes proposed with respect to honor and mutability. We ourselves were defined by our own doubts and these must be purged argued Edmund Husserl. "*What is specifically peculiar to me as ego, my concrete being as monad, purely in myself and for myself with an exclusive owness*, includes <my> every intention." [14]

By transcendental reduction to discover
the immanent laws that they obey,
animals and gods who populate
the vegetable gardens and jungles
of the cosmic sphere, dare I rest there?
Contemplating the night sky I wobble on my feet.

My music is Monadnock where I heard a haunting *Cymbeline*. Percussive tones from drums and bagpipe in shrill harmony that shattered the ancient meeting house on the banks of the Piscataquog. Phoebus, "His steeds to water at those springs" (II. iii. 22). Tuning is penetration in "horsehairs and calves-guts." [15]

Self or monad solipsistic scales.
"Putting on a rubber it's easier if you are rigid
but the routine becomes autistic repetition"[16]
By this, I came to song, copying phrases
from the various sources that lay at hand,
feeling my way
by random accident an immanent coherence
begins to manifest itself.

Upon the density of the tablets, bricks of gold,

Cartesian vortices gyrate. Today I do not exist.

Instead I follow reveries of Caribbean voyages

to a distant shore where my sons and daughters

and their children have established a concession

that sells sno-cones, blue raspberry, most desired.

The photo documents social reality and evinces

a degree of attention, appealing to subaltern minds.

A naked boy on the second floor of the courtyard,

a stairway that terminates in a blind wall.

Laundry lines simulate a safety net. Pastel light,

sublime aquamarine, masks the peeling façade.

Tenement © Donald Wellman 2011

GOD IS LOVE

I won't speculate or elaborate on this article of faith. I have no faith.
When I'm aware of the smallest dilation of blood vessels in my brain,
I know I'm in the presence of God. I seek no arguments. No code
of behavior. No personification. My philosopher heroes were
pantheists. I'm not. Neuronal pulses have generated my God.
A brain disorder. When a boy in my Edenic age
I tasted ayahuasca from a clay pot.

My boyfriend stuck his dick in my ass. Cold it was then.
The night sky parted the jungle canopy. Shadows of black on blue
on black. In the throes of young love, a godly stranger from la-la land
whispered incitements. A palisade lay among the folds of the rose.
Reason counselled desist. Love's Barons in playing card costumes,
urged me on. "Més convint le palis casser,"
as written down by Jean de Meune. When I awoke
I lay beside a stream, "a faire felde ful of folke"
lay between me and the tower. An icy wind. Jesus you squeezed
my heart and made it bitter. O tantum ergo sacramentum.
Aquinas then Ignatius of Loyola pierced my soul, incipient devotion.
George Herbert wrote, "who of the lawes sowre juice sweet wine did
[make."
I kissed the bishop's emerald ring. My Lord, I have no need of you.
"My thoughts are all a case of knives." Whence do visions arise?
On what desert shore? At the hostage exchange site an ambush befell.
Faces smeared with black grease, desert camouflage
of American origin. Sunni or Sufi? Only faces with dilated eyes.
"Poetry is complicit with death," writes Alain Badiou (54).

I began this meditation in a medieval garden.
The walls like the flesh that encapsulates the soul.
A fountain sprayed the sky with its stars, sun and moon.
I summoned the God of Love, shadows, like wings,
followed him and his footprints came so close behind

they were indistinguishable from mine. "Tan cerca vamos andando,
que el pie que mi paso aleja / viene su huella dejando."
Reading again, *Jardín cerrado,* I dream of the many trees
that are one. An innocent pulsation dilates my facial muscles,
"un sacudimiento … de donde surge el alma,"
eye sockets swell with bruised lust. Haunted by melancholy,
I played the mathematician in James Thurber's *Many Moons.*
Our next door neighbor believed in the curative power of prayer.
Her father founded the Seacoast Mission. She and her friend,
Mrs. Dale, would gather with other women around the bed
of a stricken female friend and kneel and pray
without laying on hands or audible murmuration.
The power of the psychic force which is God
was for them a healing desperation, a mute soulful entreaty.
Touching, forbidden. For my part, I testify that God resides
in the heat generated by the sense organs:
lips, penis, vagina, clitoris, eyes.
"Principles of connexion or association we have reduced to three,
namely, *Resemblance, Contiguity, and Causation;*
which are the only binds that unite our thoughts" (Hume 139).
I read "What Every School Boy Knows." Felt patronized.
Passion, unlike reason, turns man into a hunted dog
and fills a goddess with scorn. In the correspondent senses
that may be felt within the body of another
are absolute contingency and the chaos of unnamable vomit.
Even in the coarse texture of stale communion bread,
the soul may become aware of an inward thrill
that is love and it desires to communicate itself,
a happiness to be shared. Splash water on your face
and feel how the membranes of the eyelids quicken.
My God responds to a haptic touch that some share.
I am contained within an envelope like silk that secretes
a sticky goo. Sometimes like coarse wool. it produces
a rash or migraine. The nausea that arises when stones

34

are pressed against the eyes until the eye balls ache
like swollen gonads. God dwells in the taste buds.
The force that without sex or gender is a susurration
that eases painful agonies and fears that propel the brain
toward private hells. O hear my prayer, if you are or know
the gift of healing music, as is proclaimed by Pericles
in the play of that name by Shakespeare; if you are more
than the drumming in my ears that arose among the Yoruba.
When I lose my balance and fall into your embrace, hold me!

I followed a winding path through a torturous dale,
I lay beside a fountain where I read of the *Pearl.*
Her mournful father who paced the opposite shore.
Or was it an allegory by William Blake in which my spirit
had been called forth from within my ribs and took
the form of a diaphanous maid. Nonetheless philosophy
has now become set theory and I struggle to digest
the difference between "one" and the "count as one."
I learn that "where the count as one fails stands God."
Love stands in the darkness where chaos and inconsistency
form coherent statements, everywhere and nowhere, equally.

RIB BONES

Now that I've reread again the funereal *Moby Dick*
and pondered its display of gallows' humor, I ask
is it but a catalog of wry, unfounded observation?
Infectious its diction! "I am horror-struck at this antemosaic,
unsourced existence of the unspeakable horrors
of the whale, which, having been before all time,
must needs exist after all human ages are over."
Or was he before me in distinguishing "the slice
of appearance" from "the being of appearance."[17]
All my children have loved the Metropolitan Museum
and played upon the steps of the temple of Dendron
where scholars have discerned early forms of the whale.
Like Melville, I measure affect with obscure reference.
Irony denatures melancholic wit. American vitriol,
learned from a Hawthorne in the Massachusetts woods.
In my sunken wetlands, shadows replace leviathan
and serve as hooks from which depend the shrouds
or diapering clothes of the deceased and newly fledged
authors who have been cited in my monadologies
and in hymns to the God of Love. There's Robert Lowell
under his faux puritan gravestone beside his parents
in the Stark cemetery, Dunbarton, but a woodland jog
from my home. Creeley at Mount Auburn displays
commemorative pebbles atop his slab. Poets' words,
"at one with the peace that we knew in her presence,"
have memorialized deceased mothers, wives and children,
inscribed medallions for antique mementos mori.

Whispering "To Celia," in his inimitable baroque,
old Ben Jonson found at Penshurst flattering words
for his *Forests and Timbers*, epigrams that spice his *Woods*,
"Arts and Precepts availe nothing, except nature be
beneficiall, and ayding." On a misty August night

with waning moon, antique trolls in buskin
and slouch hats, capotain with ostrich feather plume,
populate the star-torn wind, mad fellows, exiled
from a Spanish court in the time of Rubens.
These my woods, not so far from those of Robert Frost,
a stile separates the graveyard from flood-control
apportioned lands. For echo I choose Emily's house
that wrinkles an earthen brow, "the Cornice in the Ground."

During the era when I sought to avoid the draft,
Vietnam in the offing, I wrote on Judgement
in *Volpone*. The duplicity of office holders
confuses meaning and truth. I desired
the death of the symbol. Set it on fire
in my private melodrama.
Gardens within gardens, animals within animals,
each fulguration of the monad instantiates eternity.
I prepare through feigned indifference for judgement day.
Nor god-ridden, nor bed ridden, I stand on the roof beam
and survey Cetus between Pisces and Eridanus,
who map the passage to the South Pole Purgatorium
on whose shores I once encountered a healing vision
of a nurse who sat at a frozen window. A gnomon
like swollen gonads. God dwells in the taste buds.
The line divides time past from time to come, itself a sail
that approached the shore and scaled a glass wall.
Countless numbers of the recently dead from Syria
and the flood plain of the Brahmaputra were stacked
in slabs upon the shore where funeral pyres shuddered
with skyward ascending sparks and the cracking of bones.
How dare the poet write of pastoral woodland tombs
amidst such slaughter? Has the poet all alone
in his house of shadows no children that require
succor and feeding? Ironic melancholy helps him

survive the titanic glare of fate-embossed night skies.
Where does the vision begin or end, thoughts
inscribed upon the waves and echoed in the stars.

He smirks as he has found another tragic metaphor,
readily at hand, another posture to assume
as affected souls leave the room and its acrid air.
He shrugs, poetry never served locally as awakening,
nor universally, in the two centuries since Edwards
at this pulpit harangued the fearful faithful with visions
of spiders suspended above the pit of hell, a sword descending
through the hollow-hearted dome of recursive dreams
that constitute their own reality, personal paranoia unpoliced
by reason or decorum as it pushes new inventions forth.
From the doldrums of the brain spring fire and ice.
Shrouds that are both lifelines and garments of the soul,
encased in hoarfrost, snap in the Antarctic winds.
Melancholy as Freud asserts knows no end.

Picasso's frightened stare from his deathbed,

grim, unshaven face that bites its lips.

My stubble a bleached white when I look

in the mirror to see if my face

is still there. Once the mercury lamp

had turned it an Oskar Kokoschka green. I cursed

my father for the bile that filled my eyes.

Part 3

WHOLE NUMBERS

I dreamed a universe of whole numbers,
Pythagorean consolation somewhere
beneath the reach of my mind,
a mackerel that glinted beyond
my grasp. Take as precept, "a singularized immanence
gives birth to the problem and resolves it
by means of contemplation." Would I were
so methodical and less self-haunted
than appears in this mixture of false
and fictionalized confessions. Once in Oregon
I owned a long serrated knife, designed
for gutting and filleting salmon. I cleaned
the blood from the blade, repeatedly
stabbing it into sand, until the metal shone.
With no one have I been able to come
clean, least with myself, never with lovers.
My spirit is vagabond, Brecht in an all-night café,
Villon adept in the argot of thieves, pandering
to corpulent men and raw recruits. Friendship
among whores as did Toulouse Lautrec.
I slept under the wall at Père Lachaise.
Since youth I have photographed gravestones,
some I could not decode, the letters hidden
under a black mold. My mother's soul.
Gamoneda's *Lápidas*, a poisonous lichen.
Secretions ooze from the rotting mass
that my town buried and groomed
with truckloads of sand to construct a football field.
Summer days, coal black rivulets
wash through the swamp
and kill the impervious alders.
I only wanted to write a coda, how did I

get here from my agonized beginning?
Can I call on those I cite for instruction?
It's the nature of collage to dissolve into bits.
Some cling to my sweater.

χῶρος

On that island lives a nation of poets
The poets have perfectly round heads with appendages
for locomotion and for lifting the objects that they daily encounter.
All of creation in that world is a living, sentient soul,
each part has a life with properties of its own.
The heavens and the planets are animals, "icons."
The gods created time in order to observe the intervals of rotation.
One living sphere revolves within another;
the head within the heart,
produces the music.
Among Yoruba as a child matures it is said to grow into its head.
Judith Butler chose to revisit the concept
of the receptacle or *chora*, that empty pouch from which all springs
with marsupial elegance. Naming of what cannot be named
is penetration and erasure, she writes (44). The receptacle
as Timaeus asserts is the nurse of all becoming.
It is a matter of translation
for becoming is always imperfect and so indeed
is translation. Among neurons, dendrites are receptors.
As used here "translation" is a process.
The chora is the mother of the ur-text that haunts her own dreams.
Are the traces of the all-father's cosmic finger
a script to be held in the hands and studied
or only smears that dissolve and become
indistinguishable from the clinamen that distributes
indissoluble substances across the night sky.
Horace declaimed the muse gave genius;
to the Greeks the power of expressing themselves
in round periods. Roman youth learn by long computation
to subdivide a pound into a hundred parts.[18]
Grais ingenium, Grais dedit ore rotundo
Musa loqui, praeter laudem nullius auaris;
Romani pueri longis rationibus

45

assem discunt in partis centum diducere.[19]
Gray ice in gaining, gray ice dead it, rotund oar.
Muse low key, pray tear lauds null us anus.
The woman who helped me from the rubber dinghy
on the Antarctic shore has been likened to a nurse.
She dispensed broad specifics, eucalyptus or mint.
I am propelled backwards by a nameless pain
associated with the loss of a body part
that takes form in my imagination
when I grieve. Tears weep from the socket from which
an eye had been surgically removed. The ghost penis
I inherited from my mother. Descend now further into the gravel pit
and scrape Sanskrit from pitted knees!
Death Valley pupfish nibble the diver's face.

φύση

Nature in its most chaotic, boundless, terrifying dimension
awakens the sublime. The failure of representation,
at its purest, first requires the apprehension of beauty (203).[20]
Shelley's salt drenched locks spread on the waves, medusae.
"I see the Deep's untrampled floor." Swirling motes
of dust and silica dispose the tired eye to close
as vision races with nausea, outpaces consciousness.
Gulps freeze time, a hammer blow between the shoulders
shocks the boy into rapt silence. Drowning faces
gaze upon the victim from empyrean heights.
In the symptom lies the symbolic reality of lost trauma (57).
I examined bent pages and underscored notes.
Concerning *Baume aus einem Stamm*, I wrote,
the trope is pillars with crowns of thorns,
cedar stumps like cacti with crowns of nails.
Magnetically charged clumps of nails. Thick
with disarray like new cut curls. Porcupine bristles.
Language failed. I could not close the distance
between the Real and its symbolization.
(Günther Uecker, *Verletzte Felder*).
I saw three penises crowned with thorns,
some bark smeared with a brown ooze.
Simply being Irish, with that gift of gab, but ignorant
of the language, might catch the falling note
where identification and misidentification collide.
On the reefs of my native island, Sergeant Major Fish
swam over domes of coral. The boys swam
to Green Cay and reveled until dawn.
On the beach of my native island,
sea wrack turned black and crunched under my boots.
A sentinel I stood in reverie,
snow pock-marked adolescent skin.

PHILADELPHIA

Lost in Philly, take me to the nearest middle school.
Take me to a shoe store, towing my daughter by her hand.
The minds of the assembled men turned toward Rome.
They sought equality among themselves and their brothers,
equal rights not justice for all would be the subject
of a delayed revolution whose time was yet
to come. A people united will not be defeated,
some said. Some died by firing squad. Some in prisons.
The profit of corporations within a corporate body
indemnified the golden rule. Profit outstrips arithmetic.
The senatorial thing to do is to have your portrait taken
in front of a bookcase. The aged poet resembled
a mother superior. "Lies lies roaches and flies"
wrote Freddie Greenfield, dedicated to John Wieners,
Amusement Business. Just think, Hemmingway owned
"A Catalan Farm." Each implement holds symbolic
intent: ax, wagon, watering can. The eucalyptus
of family lore, contains all that is Spain, all that is not.
Where is the art from Río? Where the golden mortar
and pestle? Picabia's "Women with Bulldogs" hung
in Stieglitz's Gallery 291, oily patina of sexualized nudes,
not nude at all, slathered with slippery oil, not "naked,"
not "nude," rebuff of magazine culture, but I like tabloids,
so did Freddie. Carl Van Vechten's portrait of Joyce Bryant.
Nudes for gay white men proliferate Manhattan.
Mourn the dead cavalry horses that carpet the prairie.
Wind-tossed long grass, legs and manes, aligned
with a northeasterly flow. Gouts of blood where arrows
pierce, the American flag in tatters (1881 from
a photographic account of the battle of Little Big Horn).
Did the assembled men apprehend future truths
of mutilation? Yankee doodle dandy! Stuff a cock

in a cock hat. Drive me to the next "whiskey bar,"
lackey with a plumed cockade! Shades
of "Alabama Song." The age of privilege
and decadence has just begun. The poet is a nun.
Socrates spoke, the particular doesn't warrant
the universal, "Only to beauty has it been allowed
to be most manifest" (*Phaedrus*). The bon vivant,
who like a beast proceeds to lust and procreation,
venerates "the monad of lyric poetry." The non-identity
of concept to material undoes Symbolic Order
"by magnification of the radical particular."[21]
The "new narrative" strips bare ancient bargains,
topples the soul from its throne atop the pyramid.
With aberrant, irrational lines, I lift my skirts
from the mud and fumble my way through the gap
known as Crotched Mountain, where springs flow,
a site reserved for rehabilitation. With new shoes
she cartwheels through the Zodiac, visible joy
if neighbors would douse their lights.

IMPULSE

Reading Robert Duncan's *H.D. Book*, I recover
the impulse that led to language. It was
the language of Thomas Hardy's *Jude the Obscure*
more than any other text that awakened in me
the love of poetry. I knew Latin. I'd read Virgil
and remember now Hugo's *Les chandelles du Archevêque*.
We debated where Milton stood in the hierarchy
of English poetry. I read a biography of Shelley,
the working class poet. I held that rebellion was noble,
justified by *Zarathustra*. But it was Jude
with his Gothic towers embodying beauty, the fated failure
of aspiration in his love for the very blonde,
well-spoken Sue Bridehead, the doomed attraction
to Arabella who so reminds me of a girl
from the backside of my island with whom,
at seventeen, I was ashamed to be seen. A tear of mine,
the note of my shame, was lost among stars
at the bottom of the well in my Aunt Elzada's backyard,
said to produce sweet water in time of drought.
A year later, an image in a poem by Lawson Fusao Inada
burned into my heart the desire to write my own song,
the sun that like a brilliant orange rose
over the desert of the concentration camp
where he spent his childhood. Thus I became
what I am, a melancholy expressivist, despite
intentions to employ a light touch and celebrate language
for what she loves, as if she herself were my muse.

When incident and image weigh

more than song, what then

is poetry? How much soul can

words bear? A made-thing draws

like gravity, affecting adjacencies.

It must snap like wind in the sails,

whitecaps racing loo'wards.

The cargo of perception, a mind-thing

more than a language-thing,

irreducible to words, it rides

the crests of syllables. I climb

the hill to visit winter jasmine

under an evergreen oak. Here are

souls of grandparents and Seminoles.

The philosopher unpacks his bag.

The rose will not bloom again

this year. Children in luminescent

skeleton-bone costumes celebrate

the evening of the day of the dead.

CEDAR MEN

resemble the giants of my dreams.
Gigantesque!
In his raised hands are offering cup
and tablet.
He stares upon the mountains,
his penis engorged.
My woodlands ancestors rolled
boulders down mountain walls
and built causeways across
swamps where moose feed.
You took my hand, smoothed oils
through my tired scalp.

His cap, an inverted funnel
like those of Hallstatt man.
Does our love own a future?
Her salads arrange
significant symmetries.
Heart of celery, cabbage and avocado.
A stiffness in her spine
when she dances, talk
touches the barebones of restraint.

#2
She recited Isaiah,
Bud of Jesse's branch.
Who was Judah, after all?
These questions, God,
are for you. I struggle up the hill.
My legs shake when I pause.
I am lost in snow-light
and fog-blown park lands.
Unyielding lethargy is upon me.

#3
Buses and ferries no longer run,
visits deferred.
Travelers shelter inside,
crabs in rock caves. Sepulchers.
Might as well be.
Dreamed sunlight in African skies,
souvenir of grace.
Not these. A child's smile
mimes Couperin, rondeaux.
My cuffs are sewn.
Thankful am I they don't drag
on gravel path visits to her fireside.

#4
We ran through empty movie halls,
there was no rest.
We shared eggs and orange juice.
my joy, my ruse, to live
on the fly as titmice, windblown!

#5
Like me do you hear too much Basil Bunting
in these lines? Each element of the book
pays tribute to one from whom
I have most learned. In the future I will engage
a Spinozistic perfection
as Ezra Pound hoped to do
when he spoke of gods and demi-gods
who circumvolve our minds.
We absorb where we have been
and where we're going.

Totem Poles, Museum of Anthropology, Vancouver, BC ©Donald Wellman

The light on the concrete pillars of the atrium

forms a harlequin pattern

Abstraction after Picasso, seldom playful.

Read Bergson on actualization, Deleuze recommends.

And through the plate glass

parade the timbers of the Great American Forest.

Vancouver, green against blue fields.

I seek an American baroque and it's found in Eliot's

meditative verse according to Monika Kaup.

What is the difference between meditation and thought

I asked? Is it the difference between the stasis

of trance and the pursuit of an idea

down the tunnels of the heart and its arteries.

prayer, the enabling drone?

Cedar men have figured in Jay Wright's "Boleros,"

African gods drumming on the tabla

"All names are invocations."

Crotales, cymbals, Debussy, "Pour la danseuse"

Part 4

What does Spinoza mean by "lust"?

Deadly sins plus ambition (Scholium, Part 3, Prop. 56).

These are species of emotions,

the subject is the power of the mind,

an emotion is a confused idea.

It dwells in the chora which swirls beyond percepts and perception.

It is real but not real within language, exterior to philosophy.

Pleasure is not directly bad, but good (Part 4, Prop. 41)

Joy cannot be excessive (Part 4, Prop. 42).

But melancholy, lovely melancholy, dark goddess,

you, like anguish, are evil. and a condition of the body

not just a part as are the eyes or the vulva or the penis

that suffer affliction. Do I mean addiction?

Do forces outside philosophy which is the pursuit of reason,

and therefore of the good, guide me, prod, nay whip me

to an embrace of pain as if my body were a spinning top

that wobbles on its axis and falls backwards. Precession.

My dark transport, I address the nonverbal you

in fear of being swallowed by nameless forces.

What string cuts like an ice string?

Luminous blocks of blue ice

cut from the ice shelf.

On this surface a young priest

dances in seal skin leggings

polar bear cuffs at wrists and ankles

What fish but the artic salmon

thrives in the waters of Kotzebue Sound?

Its red flesh flayed.

Donne and Eliot infiltrate

fissures of my brain.

"Ash Wednesday," is not

the act itself. Climbing

narrow stairs, my foot slips

on worn carpet. Descending

I fear falling. No vistas

here of cosmological gardens,

hedges cut in arabesques.

I approach where I hope to go

and crawl over the threshold.

In the rhapsodic pangs

of suffering transport, Donne

begs God to ravage him.

Words and meditation

revolve in separate spaces.

The words are a storm of stars.

The interior dim to insensate fingers.

The body of a woman on a butcher's slab

could be his mother. Anger turns to sadness

without salvation. The face looks

like a map of Holland, in a time of aerial

bombardment, humanoid shapes

without noses, ooze like slime molds

on a dirt floor where children cling to mothers

and mothers know from the way heads

fall away without resistance that war has

come to an end. Their kids dead.

Where two tones approach

there's an edge before they meet

as when a hair falls

over a brow and it rises

on the breath. Two lungs catch

an insubstantial whisper

between worlds. So

I thought of how I wanted

to be disposed when

I had lost consciousness.

No intervention of tubes

to feed my failing form.

No paddles to shock

a heart, no longer mine.

Do not resuscitate! Monitor

the light in my eyes!

When that margin between feeling

and fading dawns, let me collapse!

The notes collide!

MELOGRANO / POMEGRANATE

To dream becomes to write,
the location Watch House Point.
My friend owned a virgin ship
that sailed from Newport to Valparaiso.
How does a news anchor handle repetition?
Saint Edith Stein. Kids vandalized the statues.
The soul contains the body.
"The tree-combs red-gilded" Ezra Pound
(*Canto LXXIX*, 508).
He masturbates among crotales.
Crest like crust, the rooster's crown.
Priapus in the close-garden of Aphrodite.
Rose and Ayla, my daughters,
Acorn, and Hera, our mother.
Snow inters the Plaza del Grano.
"Copos," flocked snow, cotton wool
Bread from the darker seed, rye
From the oxen, blood
The poet is an ability, a machine
The BwO slips into low gear,
reverses through the sludge
of ego-involvement. Do not
count on the prayers of associates.
Measure is the rule, 'Sofreh Aghd', wedding altar
dressed with acorns, pomegranates, for fertility.
Measure lies in the exchange of freely offered goods.
She holds my hand among the market stalls
Holiday tents along the Neckar,
along a seawall near the abbey church of Lessay
where the bodies of stone fish pave the parterre.
Salvator mundi, fish, the fact of fish,
our salvation, is our life.

Balances now on the bascule scale

A diagram of measures for the dance,

participants are unable to move,

pillars planted on a sunbaked plaza

Herms where horses are tied

Priests with beard of matted rope

Mandalas lead to water-stairs

where poets and their daughters weep for beauty

my lack of periods mocks me.

CAMELLIAS

Red flowers, were they camellias?
brushed the sides of the car.
We went down a narrow lane.
Ahead lay the villa, the yard fenced
with rusted wire, the gate ajar.
My mother drove. My sex indeterminate.

Some banter, some tea. She asked,
Do you speak German, do you speak Sikh?
She had practiced in New Guinea,
among the shrunken heads. Her robe
of golden wings opened.
The feathers of an archangel.

We fled over the cattle guard gate
where the track met the country road
in the sacred grasslands of New Mexico.
I felt the heat of her flaming sword.
I lived with the cattle and goats
in a white-washed adobe
of two rooms with sky blue tin roof
on the Pacific Rim of Chiapas.

They nest within my mind, adjacent
places where memories are stored.
A thatch roofed bungalow
with dirt floors in Kenya. In each
dwells a woman and her creatures,
a small boy whose name is my own.
Take my ashes to the island
so my body may lie with my mother.

Part 5

ESCAPARATE: ELECTRODOMÉSTICOS

Knowing one masterpiece is not to know
the talent that supports daily life
and exorcised daily dissolution.
The body so thin and angular, it cannot sustain
wind or light or sails dispersed
by sun. 1955, vanishing forms that are
eaten-out blobs of grease and oil.
Feininger, Lyonel, made more than lightbirds
to ornament desert skies. He found
pollution in gnostic windmills.

I think I'll buy you a frying pan for sautéing chicken cutlets.
The coating though stained by chemical distress
will brown flesh nicely,
more tenderly than aluminum
on gas allows. When a pan heats unevenly,
droplets of grease
burst on the surface of my glasses.

Feininger's stark woodcut cathedral,
Das Manifest und Programm
                    des Staatlichen Bauhauses.
He taught woodblock printing.
The handicrafts are weaving, sewing, and cooking.
Useful arts confront entarte exhibition,
fleeing, fleeing with kids back to a New York,
more strange than Baltic fog.

I'm not sure I have reason to continue
except that he died at 101.
I have loved angular old men,
how the translucent skin covers my bones.
My father did not live so long.

The artist's feathery hands excite
the gaze that enters the "combine"
through a mirror that is a window.
Robert Rauschenberg, *Self Portrait, 1962.*
In the photograph is a wheel of tightly focused wire spokes,
a globe attached to baroque ceiling tiles
of hammered tin as in my grandmother's shop.
I intend to double down on my conclusions.
He holds the tripod as if it were a flag,
flash and face caught in art's eternal aim
to freeze duration.

My grandmother sold yarns of manifold composition,
wool and silk infused with tinsel thread of gleaming gold.
Her husband made cigars in the next room.
Tobacco dust cast its pallor on countertops and frog ponds
where promiscuous Orion bathes with his consorts.
Pleione, mother of the Pleiades,
Eos, Artemis herself. The baby in the pram
stares cross-eyed at the moon.
Which is his belt, which the sword
where the Bee Hive cluster gleams?
In the *Rudra Brahama*, it's his daughter
that he and his dog chase down the night sky,
Wave Walker, blinded by Apollo.

My children hold the rights to my post-existence,
vide the top drawer. Who brings these figures forth?
Hesiod, Callimachus, Euripides in his *Medea.*
Stella Kramrisch. Paul McCarthy with his
enormous anal plug of poisonous green.
In scattering my seed across the night sky,
I hoped to tell how life began and how it came
to mock itself as it had always done.

The soft sculpture of Hans Bellmer
guides Louise Bourgeois, polyps and phalloi
attacked by scorpions. No that's not a word.
Me and my dick will retire to the castilleti
on the beach at "basket of thorns,"
solace and beauty are left us.

Armando Reverón immersed painting in its origins.
His muñecas leak magic into the modern world.
Maja criolla, tresses crowned by the sun.
In the mountains the huts of the Mixe
are blackened by the years, the smoke,
the cycling storms. At night they disappear.

MUESTRA: NEBULOSO TENERIFE

Waiting at the airport after missing my plane to Madrid,
it turns out I was wrong on date and time.
Nothing I want to do and something
I do. I admonish myself to remember
to buy a coffee grinder. El cafecito
is my pastime. Hablé sobre lo moderno en la literatura.
A heavy book may arrive at your door.
Hold it until I return. Or a letter from the IRS.
Tell me what it contains. The agent
from the airline, when I told her
I had missed my flight, issued a new ticket.
Now I wonder. Is it Thursday or Friday?
My world clock has lost a day!
Meanwhile I'm reading Cristina Rivera Garza's
Había mucha neblina which I will give to you
when you arrive. According to her dispassionate analysis,
the greatness of Juan Rulfo lay in his being
a common man who worked carefully
with details. It's his centenary.

MUESTRA: *GUERNICA*

The different qualities of the grays in the composition
are worth noticing. Photos not allowed.
Somber gouache in neutral tones.
In some areas the surface appears smudged
as when one rubs charcoal with a finger
to give volume to a body part.
This technique is visible in a shadow on the horse's neck
and in the bodies of the five women
who populate the canvas.
It is especially true of the left thigh
of the woman who drags her disfigured torso
across the front of the room
and in the calf of her trailing right leg.
It's intentional. Unlike my parade.
I went round and round, like a helicopter,
dining at last on pasta with chorizo de Léon.
From Lavapiés to Embajadores to Atocha,
once upon a time, I had joined the crowd
leaving a rock concert during La Movida Madrileña.
That's me under the stairs in a leopard skin leotard
with feminine thighs and ass.
[Guillermo Pérez Villalta, Tarifa, Cádiz, España, 1948].
Earlier I had crossed the Black Sea with Jason
and the Argonauts in quest of the Golden Fleece.
Such I a good boy! How was I to know
the price the children would pay? Medea's rage!
Oblong faces like crusaders' shields.
Another's eyes know my secret sorrow.
Her knees press together, all in gray as before
and no make-up. Her eyes shine with naked intensity,
on that very edge of indecision, Craigie Horsefield,
Anna Moszyaska, Linhope Street, London, May 1975.

73

Last night I went into the Chinese store
around the corner and found a whisk,
luminescent orange plasticized wire loops.
Tempura chicken and cauliflower are now possible.

ESCAPARATE: BIRDHOUSE

A birdhouse teacup caddy of unknown provenance,
possibly Indonesian, made for the American
or European market. The colors are Mexican,
the birds from a Hindu fairytale. I'm on the sidewalk
my face against plate glass as in a self-portrait
by Francis Bacon. Nearby is a plaza and playground
dedicated to Mario Benedetti, "el amor pasa por los parques
casi sin verlos amándolos." In the new flamenco,
the instrumentation includes piano and saxophones,
merging jazz, salsa and reggaetón, even a kettle drum
supplements the cajón, and always the necessary
chasquido and castanets. If absence has value
for some to play with a conjunto from Xalapa does.
The boys in white traje with small guitars, son jarocho.

ESCAPARATE: THE MILL

The coffee mill stood in the barn for generations before my time.
Its orange wheels like locomotive parts.
A battered tin chalice or hopper
for an iconic dream, never materialized by my ancestors.
Like Tantalus, I'd turn the wheel in a dry goods store
of the future. Swirls of psychedelic light
fill the room. At hand are rounds
of hard white cheese, large knives with scimitar blades,
bolts of coarse linen for aprons and bandages.
During the Spanish American War, my great grandfather
was said to have been meat cutter and socialist.
Surveying the hardware stores of an alien city,
I derive pleasure from machines for slicing eggs and
wands that will bring water to a boil.
Do eggbeaters exist as of old, square blades
in a cylindrical world? Do dogs bark
when they sense a presence at the door?
I am startled by a presence just outside
that moves against the dark. Wheels and cogs
in the escaparate at Barclay's mime functionality.
The boy on the train claimed he spoke English.
He did not. Malformed teeth, thin legs and pure joy
in his demeanor. Where does it start?
Duchamp and I are attracted to sad young men,
a melancholy ghost who is an alter ego.
The rhymes chanted during recreo
cited a poem addressed to Teresita. [14 Feb. 1927].
A lizard and his wife dance and cry and laugh.
The retired professor lived on for many years
after the rape of his daughter, as he had to do,
unable to salvage an era of unredeemed suffering.
Old friends passed and teeth failed, but the pattern

of the sand that filtered through the woven basket
where it rested in the courtyard was a spiral of red molecules
as if the post-human galaxy might appear on the horizon
at any time or already had, although the swirling abyss
was no longer able to meet the needs of daily life.
Lentils and beans and a touch of oil to ease the bowels,
a rug to place over knees. I have fused "Endgame"
and "The Snows of Yesteryear," Beckett and Villon,
Mais où sont les neiges d'antan? Overnight
the climate swings from boiling hot to artic gales,
dismantling governments and erratic dreams.
And yet there is glee among children, pushing
and shoving and jumping rope. My heart lifts
as if to welcome an acknowledged land.

Mi corazón se eleva
cuando subo la escalera
a ver las estrellas.
Dicen "vete, vete"
a la frontera muy fuera.
Allá habría
luz y algo a comer.
Desnúdate y baila.

And these words were quiet thunderclaps
as my hands massaged my hands
and I began to set the stage for a game of chess
to be played on a tennis court
with giant figures, lemon-yellow, fluorescent pink.

Sometimes at night

you lie by my side

and press yourself

lightly against me.

You takes my penis

and caress it.

No more than that.

Blonde angel

with boyish breasts.

Even pregnant

you come to me

and I taste your mouth.

Las Palmas are closer to Casablanca than Madrid.

Mantua is closer to home than New York City.

I have met you in the street

and in my bed.

To write as love compels a force its own.

DEREK WALCOTT, 1930-2017

Of how many can it be said that he or she broke ground
and what does it signify? A metaphor
drawn from the ceremonies of construction
or is something more subtle and enduring intended
as in breaking bread during the vernal equinox?
I mourn the death of a poet whose smile bespoke
generations of gentleness, reaching back through slavery
to the shores of Africa. His smile wrinkled
with watching the waves merge with the sand
and the horizon meld with the sea.
The soft gray hair of his face
signified warmth and love, not sarcasm.
On the roof of a church in the village where I lived,
the American flag was stretched like a target
for aerial bombardment in order to indict
the colonialism of the Vietnam era.
Time is a bleached rag on the clothesline of history.

"That sail which leans on light," six monosyllables
register a world as percept and gnomon in the tides of time.
The book is never nearly done

even as words seek redemptive silence.

Part 6

Books upon the table. Bookshelves line walls.

Honeycomb the hive. Windows too are books,

now open on a summer meadow. A soul

slips over waterfalls and silken pillows,

canoes moored on banks of slow philosophy

where acolytes theorize reciprocity. My sister self,

your castanets trace arabesques. Stairs whisper

refrains to stones laced with greeny moss.

Bannister troughs host rivulets of marigolds.

A star rises among stanzas of doubled rhyme.

My peasant child, my Columbine, follow me,

the shepherd cries, to a land upside down

of mushrooms and acorns. Lament. For this day

a poet closed his book. His lyre floats away.

His coronet no longer sounds. His chaplet

withers, Orpheus, undone by sad measures.

Shepherds and daughters of Arcadia, know how

mares foal and ewes give milk without aid

of aimless meter. Instead couple as couplets do.

The pollen of the butter cup is your sweet suck!

THE GENEROSITY OF THE DEAD

I
The purpose: dissemble / disassemble. One is prose,
the other poetry. All commentary is sadistic.
Will prayer attain the intimacy of a conversation with god?
Like those once imagined by John of the Cross
in the trans-historical baroque.

So much depends on discipline / disciplines
... *so lovely sucking theory from doubts* (*Debbie* line 498)

"Now I occupy the design," the last words of Lisa Robertson's
Rousseau's Boat incite my interrogation of the baroque.

The "generosity of the dead" is our problem, she writes.
When poets rhymed, our Meditations followed the Discipline
[of Ignatius Loyola,
Eliot's *Ash Wednesday* is Neo-Baroque beggary / buggery, I cried.
Spiritual quest in a rationalized world.
She confesses, "dominant I wanted to wear memory like a
[molded hunger"
(*Lisa Robertson's Magenta Soul Whip* 11).
Her readings defy narrative clarity.

Poetry disdains the talking cure.
The poet constructs the many-layered fable, etude and exercise.

In the visual arts, Matisse's decorative figures are
exquisite ornamental exercise.
In Caravaggio's paintings the Baroque eschewed black.
Velasquez sought to mirror virtuality.
The painter inhabits design — displays severed heads.
Old John Gower addressed the heads on the walls of Antioch.

Shakespeare's baroque theater
calls forth the Duke of Dark Corners, like a spider, *Measure for*
[*Measure*,
a problem play that is an unfolding of multiple plots,
contests the Counterreformation and its particular Baroque.
Police work for the soul.
Seething Angelo.

II
Woven ropes of chastisement mock penalty of law
Robertson is polymorphous.
"Into many sexes slowly pivoting like leaves"

She is language.
"Glossy black notebook with red-ink-edged pages, water
[dampened" (*R's Boat* 23).
She is her notebooks (there are four) ...
Ancient trope of page and leafage, modesty of decorative
elegance

Canal boat reveries, the dreaming barque.
She pivots as she reads in her exploration of personhood
(*R's boat* 23).
What does Debbie learn from R?[22]

Not that the poet's identity perishes with his body. Instead his
mind merges with that of God with whom it was always united
without memory from time immemorial. Rousseau's state of na-
ture is a fable for a Spinozist. Spinoza's immortality seeks not to
preserve individuality.

"The mirage of soul skims the trees" (*Debbie* line 50)
"Duration isn't singular." (*3 Summers* 58)

III

Indexical and melancholic, the *tristess* of masturbation.

"You want to enter into the humility of limitations
"Coupled with exquisite excess" ("The Present," *R's Boat*, 27)
Goat foot, gout foot
I'm reading several poets in the same "meanwhiles"[23]

"So I attended vegetation
"Where ornament is unfinished
"And it was a purely melancholic ritual" ("A Cuff," *R's Boat*, 39).

The flamboyant's long scabbards rattle
Hay Cadáveres, I cry!

Indeed, so runs the dream that riffles the hairs on my neck
My legs tire
I prepare a ragout of exquisite beef

So louche
Legs splayed

"A pink city doesn't rise from the forest" (*R's Boat*, 65). In Freud's reading, Dora understood the geography of sex, engorged *nymphae*, framing a lake. Otherwise there were dense forests and a path along the shore, nettles …

The tenderness of my monolog may offend
The heady scent of ripened fruit

Elsewhere she writes, "Your name is a syllable on my face and I speak it from your own juice" ("Hydromel" or mead) (*The Men* 31).

Another period of snow and drizzle, spring delayed, and soon the runners, male and female, will surge over the hills, looking for sun, spurred by the panic of gunfire.

My sidereal gender wanders among the stars
as the earth's orthogonal axis precesses
during a year of 25,800 days.
Soon fish will leave the sea
and Aquarius will restore balance to the night.
That's disco! Daddy!
When I was a kid,
I glued stars to my ceiling.
Wolves prowl. No true astronomy secures doubt.

IV
Ed Foster's *Sowing the Wind* makes a lucid statement on "material" or "physical gnosis." Observation and perception "teach" a higher order of knowing, but no transcendental order is proposed, no dogma, only the certainty of what Husserl once called an intuition.

A truth beyond self-evident solipsism.

Lisa is more accident prone than other poets.
Not more so than am I. We both like inversions.
Meaning slices and comforts.
Her method pursues prosody.
"I wanted the phonemes to spread around me like a sea"
(*R's Boat* 17).
Elusive logics emerge like spawning salmon or girls on a lawn

The howling disturbs my sleep.
Bear claws sculpted into the muck of a forest trail.
Ed would not turn down this path as I have done.

"He'd hone his questions
"showing us that grammar
"yields the answer" (12)
It's an ironic and serene gnosticism
"strong young men,
"not Nazi's,
"to join him
"in that mountain hut" (13)

These are love poems,
"If you'd just turn
"one final thrust
"of that ecstatic storm
"would make us what we are." (39).

In sight and sound
lies true gnosticsm
not denial.

"I am the words you seek and say" (41).

IV
"Dwelling" makes authentic existence possible.[24]
A slow philosophy endeared Martin Heidegger
to boys who visited him on Todtnauberg.

Hütte, a hut or refuge in a technological age.
Paul Celan crossed the killing fields / waldwasen
to meet the philosopher
whose "star die" sat on the rim of the well.

Jeremy Prynne theorizes, as universal to poetry, a writing frame-
work that intersects with the existing world order and flirts with
narcissism, activating a system of discontinuities and breaks

which interrupt and contest the intrinsic cohesion and boundary
profiles of its domain so that there is constant leakage inwards and
outwards across its connections with the larger world order.[25]

The canoe is a dwelling within a watery world.
A framework for philosophers.
On which side of the night does love leave its whispering
                                    [moccasin prints.
Prynne proposed to "refluidize for soluble modularity."

My family kept cattle; my grandfather was a butcher
In my own youth, I stumbled on roots near a cairn in Uhland's
                                    [upland,
a hint of eyebright sprouting from the moss
where I would lie me down today
and contemplate mares' tails,
skying blades of tufted grass.

Poets dwell in graveyards.
Choughs squawk!

V
My fall into a lyric mode consorts with abjection
Bodies and landmines lie in the fields.
Hay cadáveres
Mosul, Orlando
and clog the putrid waters of the anal canal.

"Hurricanes flare up impatiently flinging our furniture and debris
onto our physical identities. Our roles in society
are attacked by what we own.
[Carla Harryman, *Adorno's Noise* 14]

The poet is a flaneûr; the essayist is wary of conclusions.
To my nose, the scent of flowers does not nauseate
so much as does the stench of sardony. It hovers in rainclouds
over water lilies.
I cannot make more of such perfume
than to associate the grappling of the roots
with shit and blood.

Lucio Fontana revealed the substance of color when he slit the
                                                              [canvas.
Poets and artists "tear open the firmament itself,
to let in a bit of free and windy chaos
and frame in sudden light the vision that appears through the rent.
Wordsworth's spring or Cezanne's apple,
the silhouettes of Macbeth or Ahab" (*What is Philosophy* 205).
Why do I feel nauseated?
Who is a Nazi, who is not?
Banana leaves carpet banana tents.

The strictures of reciprocal love
brought me to a fusion of Simone de Beauvoir and Robert Duncan
who wrote of a prosody where "Each syllable of the poem,
if we keep alive each sound in the sounding of the whole,
is such a stricture—just the sound it is—that proves
in the movement of the poem to be a liberation."[26]

"Where Nurses of Perfidy chant, as they descend to earth
'Feed from my tongue
  'Touch my wet hip
    'Give me words
      'Give me words'"
(*Debbie an Epic*, 60).

Do you see the canoe in the stars, Donny?
The bubbles in the muck?

This a love poem.
Lisa Robertson writes of "we who have no memories at all."
(*Three Summers*, 16)

Sex loses its generic markers and finds convoluted form. The tree
that is a phallus is also the vegetative root of human reproduc-
tion. Fish, serpents and manatees populate the mind stirred by
voluptuosity.

The dripping house went dark and the forest began, availing it-
self of the lunations of the little goat and the needle, the slow
interweaving dance or reproductions that need the dew. Now
the manatee had reached the grass and moving its thick pectoral
fins crept toward the stone seat, crawling with the slippery ease
its oiled skin gave it. (Lezama Lima, *Paradiso*, 49).

Allegorical manatees bathe on the shores of my lingering.

VI
What then is the American Baroque? For this is my nominal
                                                    [subject.
Surreal among the mangroves, where lizards and apes, typewriters
and crocodiles lay their larvae
and salt water is purified.
Taino or Penobscot direct the prehensile mind
through tarred and knotted ropes of melancholy?

Extermination and deluded hope are married to wilderness.
As in other romantic tales, the downy bodies of newborn babes
haunt the shelves in storage rooms.

Hay cadáveres! Néstor Perlongher's
lament for Argentina in the time of the Generals.

"In the nets of fishermen
"In the tumbling of crayfish
"In the bit of hair that is nipped
"In a small unfastened hair clip
"Hay cadáveres!"

Ethos impinges on style:
"Now I'm thinking that all along it's been my body
"that I don't understand." (*Three Summers* 62).

For all my sardony, I do not laugh.

I weep with resolution.

Cod / ling my gray fish, gay fish.

Part 7

CONJURY

Words and constellations catch my eye.
Prospero, I inscribe *galaxias.*
Con cada resolución, I cry.
The practice is neither deliberate
nor random. After all
my mind has shaped the environment
that sustains my habits.
Poems in German upon the piano.
Enchantments of a girl,
Da stieg ein Baum. O reine Übersteigung!
O Orpheus singt! O hoher Baum im Ohr![27]
I'm lost. Dante has wormed his way
among couch cushions. I wanted foamy lace
as when a dolphin plunges in azure that ripples
its swathe through indigo seas.
Internal programming prompts me to assess
what is relevant to poetry's advance;
by way of whim something old comes to mind
that I long claimed as mine.
Never truly understood.
"The poem is the cry of its occasion,"
Wallace Stevens expostulates.[28]
Yellow-green moss where waste water trickles,
a rivulet at the edge of the garden
seeps into the field of vision.
How it is that these observations
stir perception or burn their affect into mind is
at best fortuitous, as if nymphs
and demigods supervised moonrise harvest.
Surprise blindsides the soul.
"El tiempo tiene un cuerpo invisible, es la eternidad."[30]
On the margin of the stream of thought,

I had hoped to find a resting place
for melancholy and there it was,
staring me in the face,
"Time has an invisible body, it is the soul."

Straining for amazement, serial composition
anticipates its end. Sparks within a penumbra.
Seated among hydrangeas the musician finds chords
unknown to me. Alberto Marsicano.
"O organismo quer perdurar" (Décio Pignatari).
These the conjunto that populates
the clouds above the meadow, a strumming
in the rye and nodding blades of wheat grass
unleash lacy jags of semen.
Sleep sweet sleep, heavy eyes.
Careening faciality studies itself.
Amazed, Emily Dickinson
nestles herself in my pubic hair.
Need it be visceral to be real?
Or is it only the resistless rhapsody
of a night song that overwhelms decorum?

Dislocated melancholy, is this the sad loss that brings tears?

Or is it the small portion of sustenance that enables

mental excursions? Images of reconciliation as when

fathers recognize their daughters, a soap opera

like *King Lear*. Once in an imaginary apprenticeship,

I was understudy to the fool. My voice cracked when I plead

with the king to have mercy on himself

before he waged war on friends and allies.

Now I wonder about the words

I have prepared. Have they served to elevate my spirit?

Do they bring solace to yours as you sit there, my son, harried

                                        [by the demands

of children. The snow that will not release the year

to its purpose prevents our meeting

as too often it has done.

ENCLOSURES

On a tag of paper, once a bookmark, I read, "Enclosures as stated"
–the paper has yellowed. The edge that protruded from
the book is ragged and brown, burnt by exposure:
air, light and the indifferent toxins found
in rooms where the book has resided, shelves
like plateaus negotiated on a journey of decades
through apartments and woodland cottages
where children were raised to their different ends.
"Enclosures as stated" indicates attachments.
The purpose from which these words descend
now lost, but the reminder surfaces repeatedly
as I rummage for a memory of its provenance.
Were the supposed "enclosures—therapeutic or mercenary,
of legal or contractual import? "Enclosure," singular,
suggests a garden or pens where goats or cows are kept,
"enclosed" within "enclosures," the stone walls provide
shelter from wind. Plus ca change, they say, a life
not lived. *Jardín cerrado*, as if there were only one
but populated by moonlight and silver fountains.
The clacking of olive leaves, "that which gleams
and does not gleam" γλαύξ, γλαυκῶπις, (LXXIV 458).
On those seas, the enclosed man begged grace from god,
are gebideð. The island submerged like a whale,
the morning of a resurrection without hope.
Enclosures like prison cells constrict the dreaming heart
at the very moment of its doomed sojourn.
"Enclosures," penalties, no doubt, and "as stated"
implies a lack of alternatives, the true knell
of doom and its encumbered language. Thought,
averse to consequences diverts itself with puzzles,
poems, hallucinogenic experiments. What promises
of forgotten satisfactions are most at stake? Or not?

CONTRADICTORY SENTENCES

form series of indeterminate length. Energy
arises in bending the line. Abrupt
carriage returns. Word substitutions.
Staging motivates scaled unfoldings.
"When you look at / the fieldwork, you see
the problem of agency supported by
/ the sophistication of upward mobility
… A contrapuntal / structure moves among
several different lives." A cue to the method
of writing. The world order under capitalism.
The method generates incongruities
in the field of action. Meaning is in play,
"an abyss of crop-duster dictums" writes
Andrew Levy, *Artifice in the Calm Damages*,
the chapbook from which I have been quoting.
He continues "revolutionaries / via minor routes,
filth, blood, and noise." His text, in the key of anarchy,
no newly born utopia looms on the far horizon
of destruction. Alice Notley, in turn, writes,
in the key of really pissed off. "Most of us
are slaves, largely by consent. Or / you could say
we're brainwashed." She's sardonic.
"I work / in a shelter for battered women.
I submitted to / a pharaonic circumcision."
Facing the abyss of embodied affect,
paralyzed, I see a cat sprawled under the clothes tree.
Juan Goytisolo muere en Marrakech,
city of highlife nightmare, jùjú music,
Djemaa el fna, central square of dance parties
and all night food stalls, estranged from myself,
grizzled old man in a brilliant Berber jacket.
Goytisolo sat with his back to the wall. Mint tea.

a notebook for recording phrases from an Arabic
that has no alphabet, seeking to better understand
those with whom he shared his exile,
three adopted children and their mother.
The tide that surrounds us grows impatient
with lame-foot measures. He chose
the Atlantic shore at Larache for his internment.
He eschewed literary prizes. From the need
to educate his children, he accepted the Cervantes,
crippled as he was and unable to stand on his legs.
Now he lies with Jean Genet as he had wanted.

Exile is central to my disposition. Abjection,
docility and submissiveness, threaded as they are
with anger, inform the only poetry any of us write.
Remember Alice's magic! Is it possible
to be an American in an age of deception?
That's motive for exile in hers, in my case.
In Andrew's? what does he do? He is pushed
toward the book. He begins with a conclusion,
"Nothing is in here." Title and first line
of an earlier composition. By that he means
all that once had embodied joy is now absent.
Such desolation! Humor doesn't help.
"The vile stench makes sunbathing impossible
and swimming / through the slime ... the tiny
trapped sea creatures living inside perish
/ when the algae hit the beach, creating
a putrid sulfurous stench." Is there a resolution
to "The chaos of Dreaming Life" where poetry
is wed with pain? Alice writes, "I wish
you'd waterboard me. Make my heart crash.
We're immortal. It hurt my throat. What a bunch
of liars they are." She has no interest "in being myself.

I just am." She forces the poet's hand, "There's
nothing here now, there is only me." She has
no answer to hovering incompleteness, "It isn't
a good price that you pay for writing a poem."

Everyone I know has money for their daily needs.
Even more than they know. To them, within the confines
of their reality, there's no imaginable alternative
to their security and comfort. This insight
came to me during a heatwave. Even for my kids,
there's nothing to be done but to call the installer.
"I tried to learn how to be a person," Alice wrote.
"In death we speak, in dreams we speak, / and
in the immaterial past and future our vocal cords
are fast as birds." She clutches a grail of light
to her chest and gives it to a child. So too thought
those in honor of Goytisolo as his bark rode the waves.
He no longer had words for his life. Andrew concludes,
"These are my words. Nobody asked me to write them."
As to the riddle of this essay-poem, he suggests,
"You could identify with the poor." That's
the key of Juan's attempt to decode
the analphabetism of the crowded square.[29]

Wrapped in folds of uncertainty

The prospect of affection caused Boethius to tremble

Impossible to be so naked

He hugged his knees

A limpet attaches herself to my heart.

Hopefully she won't metastasize.

Yes Robert Frost is a great poet.

But, each wins love for different reasons.

That damn limpet gnaws.

To win, to earn, to fall –

very illogical. Vallejo's widowed wine bottle.

My daughter calls it sleep training,

steeling yourself not to run when the baby cries.

I'd like to say, yes, it's only a matter

of unpleasant odors, viscous fluids, but because

of the limpet, I shrink into myself.

That calcined creature will not let loose.

My instinct lay with the automaton

not the ape, nor the age.

She came on like "riverrun."

Her limbs fused, descending stairs.

She chats and she chats.

She is our mother, mother of us all.

Phonemes today, in their discourse,

contaminate one another.

Stars spangle the night sky.

So is the American Pastoral

set in now foreclosed Grover's Corners,

anywhere USA.

The prayers of the republic

swathed in Gothic melancholy.

So was a time before the Wars.

So was time before Vietnam.

Not for the first time boys and girls

lay down in different lands far from home,

places that can no longer be found.

A meridian that is the site of a conversation.

Poetry must, like philosophy, speaks with its other.

ENDNOTE

"The essay, however, does not let its domain be prescribed for it. Instead of accomplishing something scientifically or creating something artistically, its efforts reflect the leisure of a childlike person who has no qualms about taking his inspiration from what others have done before him. The essay reflects what is loved and hated instead of presenting the mind as a creation ex nihilo on the model of an unrestrained work ethic. Luck and play are essential to it." Theodor W. Adorno, "The Essay as Form," *Notes to Literature*, V.1. Trans. Sherry Weber Nicholsen (New York: Columbia University Press, 1991) 3-4.

NOTES ON THE TEXT

[1] I mark these images as beacons for my navigation. The first lines reference architectural studies undertaken by López Carmona in order to balance the crumbling facades of the *Catedral Metropolitana de la Asunción de la Santísima Virgen María a los cielos* before the stones inevitable plunge into the crypt of the Aztec *Templo Mayor* upon which they stand. In Prolog Pages (Chiba-Ken, 2009), I wrote, the lines that follow. I have corrected the phrase "hyperbolic parabola" to read "hyperbolic paraboloid."

[2] José-Luis Moctezuma, *Spring Tlaloc Séance* (Chicago : Projective Industries, n.d.) 11.

[3] Maria Zambrano, "El vegetal," Roma 1954, *Algunas lugares de la pintura*, Madrid 1991 (Reprinted in *Cuba secreta*, ed. Jorge Luis Arcos, Colección ensayo, no. 90. Madrid, 1996: 148-49) Tr. Donald Wellman.

[4] Micah Ballard, *Afterlives* (Oakland: Bootstrap Press 2016) 83.

[5] Gottfried Wilhelm Leibniz, *Discourse on Metaphysics and the Monadology*. Tr. George R. Montgomery (NY: Prometheus, 1992) 15.

[6] Cole Swenson. *Ours* (Berkeley: U. Cal. P, 2008) 26.

[7] Leibniz "Monodology" in Montgomery op. cit. The numbers are Leibniz's paragraph numbers.

[8] Antonio Ochoa. "¿cuando tú estabas en el sótano, yo estaba muerto?" *Él toro de Hiroshima*. (Mexico: Mangos de Hacha, 2016): 28

[9] *INRI* (Madrid: Visor 2004) 29.

[10] Farad Showghi, *End of the City Map.* Tr. Rosmarie Waldrop (Providence: Burning Deck, 2003).

[11] Adapted without registering line endings from John Beer's *Lucinda: A Poem* (Ann Arbor: Canarium, 2016) 188.

[12] Paul Klee. Notebooks, Vol. 1, *The Thinking Eye* (20).

[13]
      Her vomit full of bookes and papers was,
      With loathly frogs and toades, which eyes did lacke,
      and creeping sought way in the weedy gras:
      Her filthie parbreake all the place defiled has.
                    The Faerie Queene, Canto I, XX.

[14] Edmund Husserl. *Cartesian Meditation.* Tr. Dorion Cairns (The Hague: Nijhoff, 1960).

[15] So argued Charles Fussell before the performance of his *Cymbeline* by the Monadnock Music Sinfonietta, dir. Gil Rose, Francestown, NH, Old Meeting House, July 28, 2016.

[16] Misha Pam Dick. *This is the Fugitive* (Essay Press, 2016) 15.

[17] Alain Badiou, *Being and Event*, 124.

[18] C. Smart and by E. H. Blakeney (*Horace on the Art of Poetry,* [London: Scholartis Press, 1928]).

[19] Q. Horatii Flacci "Ars poetica," 323-326.

[20] Slavoj Žižek "…nature in its most chaotic, boundless, terrifying dimension … is best qualified to awaken in us the feeling of the Sublime." *The Sublime Object of Ideology* (NY: Verso, 1989).

21 From Barrett Watten's discussion of the New Sentence and the New Narrative in *Questions of Poetics* (Iowa 2016) 99-103.

22 Steve Evans has pointed out that Robertson's use the boat is as a vehicle for transportation into reverie beyond the shores of purposeful existence. *Jacket* 2005, http://jacketmagazine.com/27/evan-robe.html.

23 A "meanwhile" is neither a part of time nor an aspect of the eternal. It is a form of becoming. The virtual is actualized during a "meanwhile." It is a paradigm for the actualization of the sacred. "All meanwhiles are superimposed on one another, whereas times succeed one another" (WIP 158). In the visual arts and poetry, planes, stacked on top of one another, with variations in degree of overlap, construct the vertical dimensions of a poem that might otherwise be understood as serial in its composition, functioning as montage does but without the depth wherein beauty often lies. Beauty is immanent to this concept. Deleuze and Guattari define "beauty" as "sensation." They conclude this section of *What is Philosophy*, subtitled, "Philosophy, Science, Logic, and Art," with this remark, "Philosophy is always meanwhile" (159). Visualize the interface between planes in the work of Pound or Mira Schendel as spatial approximations of the concept of "meanwhile." Consider what Luce Irigary meant when she wrote, "We need to proceed in such a way that linear reading is no longer possible (80). Gilles Deleuze and Félix Guattari, *What is Philosophy* (NY: Columbia, 1993), cited as WIP.

24 *Slow Philosophy*, Michelle Boulouse Walker (London: Bloomsbury, 2017). My contrast is from an early note on Paul Celan's "Todtnauberg" by Pierre Joris (1988) http://wings.buffalo.edu/epc/authors/joris/todtnauberg.html.

25 Poetry Reading by Jeremy Prynne, University of Chicago 2009 https://www.youtube.com/watch?v=rjM8SruqTdo.

26 *The Truth and Life of Myth* (Freemont: Sumac, 1968) 67.

27 Rainer Maria Rilke, *Die Sonette an Orpheus*

28 Wallace Stevens, "An Ordinary Evening in New Haven."

29 Cited texts: Andrew Levy, *Artifice in the Calm Damages* (Victoria TX: Chax, 2017); Andrew Levy, *Nothing in Here* (NY: Eoagh, 2011); Alice Notley, *Certain Magical Acts* (NY: Penguin, 2016).

30 Lezama Lima, "Revelaciones de mi fiel Habana" (1949).

31 "Octavio Paz," *Fragmentos de su imán.*

ABOUT THE AUTHOR

DONALD WELLMAN is a poet and translator. He has trans-
lated books of poetry by Antonio Gamoneda, Emilio Prados,
Yvan Goll, and Roberto Echavarren. *Albiach / Celan: Reading
Across Languages* is from Annex Press (Spring 2017). His *Expres-
sivity in Modern Poetry* is forthcoming from Fairleigh Dickinson
University Press. His poetry has been described as trans-cultural
and baroque. His collections of poetry include *Roman Exer-
cises* (Talisman House, 2015), *The Cranberry Island Series* (Dos
Madres, 2013), *A North Atlantic Wall* (Dos Madres, 2010), *Pro-
log Pages* (Ahadada, 2009), and *Fields* (Light and Dust, 1995).
As editor of O.ARS, he produced a series of annual antholo-
gies including *Coherence* (1981) and *Translations: Experiments in
Reading* (1984).

OTHER BOOKS BY DONALD WELLMAN
PUBLISHED BY DOS MADRES PRESS

A NORTH ATLANTIC WALL (2010)
THE CRANBERRY ISLAND SERIES (2012)

HE IS ALSO INCLUDED IN:
REALMS OF THE MOTHERS:
THE FIRST DECADE OF DOS MADRES PRESS - 2016

FOR THE FULL DOS MADRES PRESS CATALOG:
www.dosmadres.com